Simple Guide to Modern Calligraphy & Creative Lettering

FOR BEGINNERS

Workbook with Practice Pages and Fun

© Copyright 2020 - All rights reserved.

The contents of this book may not be reproduced, duplicated or transmitted without direct written permission from the author.

Under no circumstances will any legal responsibility or blame be held against the publisher for any reparation, damages, or monetary loss due to the information herein, either directly or indirectly.

Legal Notice:
You cannot amend, distribute, sell, use, quote or paraphrase any part of the content within this book without the consent of the author.

Disclaimer Notice:
Please note the information contained within this document is for educational and entertainment purposes only. No warranties of any kind are expressed or implied. Readers acknowledge that the author is not engaging in the rendering of legal, financial, medical or professional advice.

INTRODUCTION

Since a very young age I had a fascination for these beautiful letters and patterns and I was very determined to practice them until I managed to make them flow and use them as part of my artistic expression.

We all have so much magic within us and there are so many ways to express it, and I hope to help you achieve it as well and to experience all the magic that I found.

In this book I have decided to compile only the basic information, so you can start right away on this beautiful path and express all your creativity and originality.

I hope you thoroughly enjoy it.

Let's begin!

Available now on Amazon

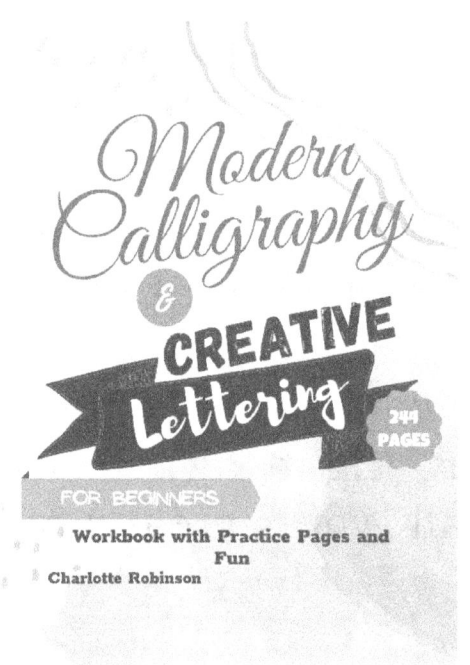 

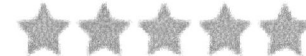

PAPERBACK ASIN: B08DSX3J9J

This **"Modern Calligraphy and Creative Lettering for beginners: Workbook with Practice Pages and Fun"** is a complementary workbook, which contains:
- Templates to practice the basic strokes.
- Basic alphabet with uppercase and lowercase templates.
- Ten beautiful styles of letters (including an alphabet, numbers, words and positive phrases).
- More than 180 great words and phrases, and designs of the lettering art to practice and have fun.

1
FIRST STEPS

BASIC TERMINOLOGY

It is very common today to hear terms like Calligraphy and Lettering without knowing what they mean or how they differ. Well, we will start by knowing what each one means:

Calligraphy

CALLIGRAPHY, is more than a beautiful handwriting, is the art of forming beautiful symbols by hand and arranging them well to show integrity y harmony. It is about perfecting the motions of your pen.

Lettering

LETTERING, refers to drawing or illustrating letters where the letters become an expression of art. It is everything to do with the formation and use of alphabet letters to communicate meaning, and so it involves typography, sign-writing, graffiti, graphic design and many other disciplines.

BOOST YOUR CALLIGRAPHY SKILLS

We will start by learning what the basic strokes are and how to do them. It is very important to practice each of these strokes, this will allow you to feel comfortable when starting with the other templates.

Let's learn more about the basic strokes and what skills will help us enhance:

Up strokes help you to practice light pressure, making thin lines . It´s important to get a consistent line that looks smooth and not shaky.

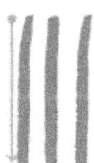

Down strokes help you to practice more pressure, making thick lines.

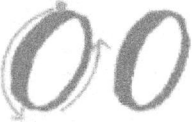

Ovals help you to practice an important shape for letters as a, b, d, etc., making a thick down stroke and a thin up stroke.

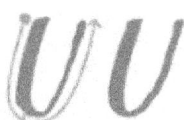

Under turns help you to practice a round shape without the closing loop, making a thick down stroke and a thin up stroke.

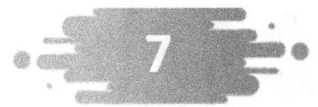

Over turns help you to practice a round shape at the top, making a thin up stroke and a thick down stroke.

Descending Loops help you to practice a shape for letters as j, making a long down stroke and a thin up stroke loop.

Ascending Loops help you to practice a shape for letters as t, making a thin upstroke loop and a thick down stroke.

So, let's begin with the basic strokes.

BASIC STROKES

Up strokes

BASIC STROKES

Up strokes

Now try it one more time without the gray guide. Let's practice.

BASIC STROKES

Down strokes

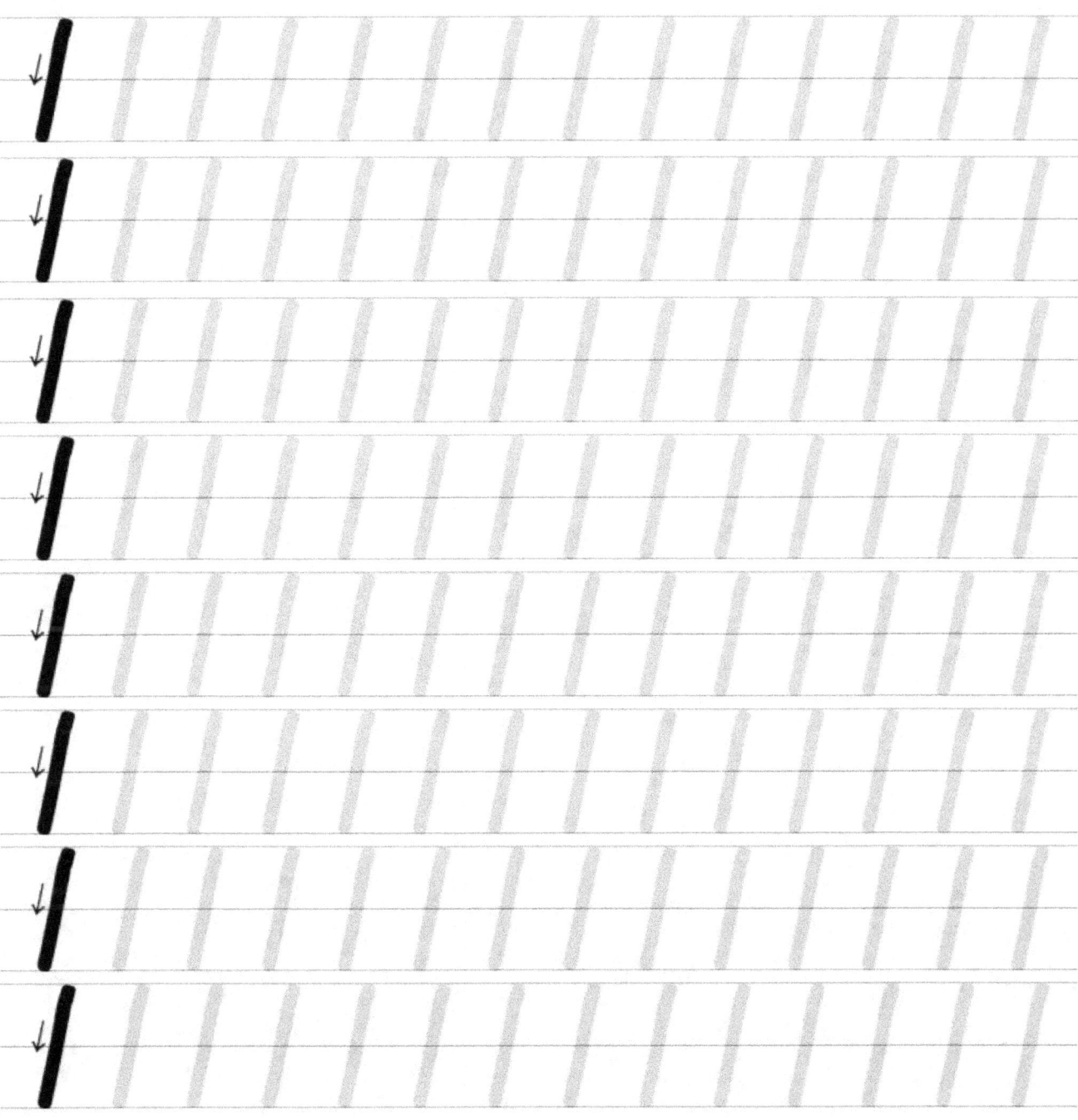

BASIC STROKES

Down strokes

Now try it one more time without the gray guide. Let's practice.

BASIC STROKES

Ovals

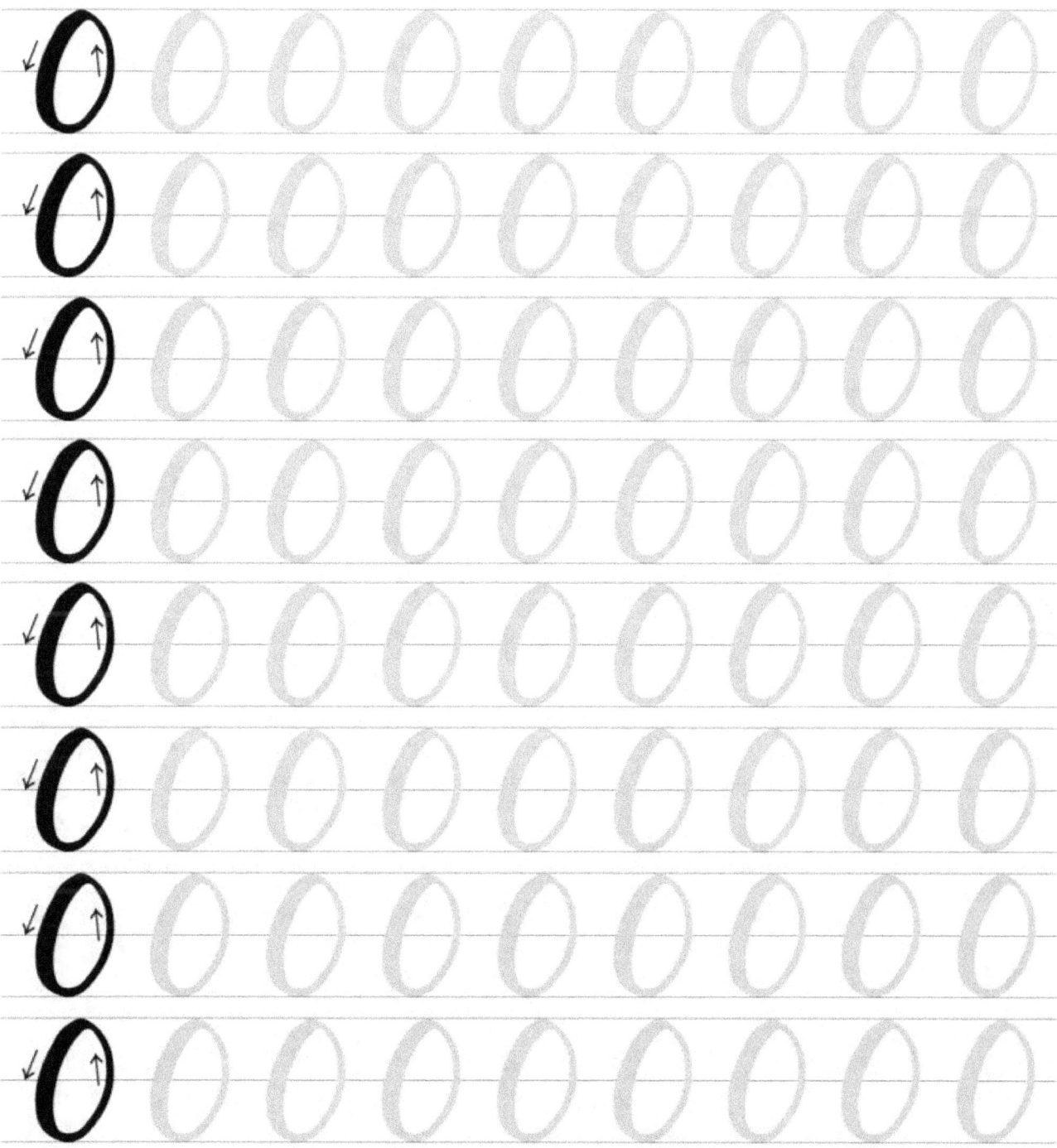

BASIC STROKES

Ovals

Now try it one more time without the gray guide. Let's practice.

BASIC STROKES

Under Turns

BASIC STROKES

Under Turns

Now try it one more time without the gray guide. Let's practice.

BASIC STROKES

Over Turns

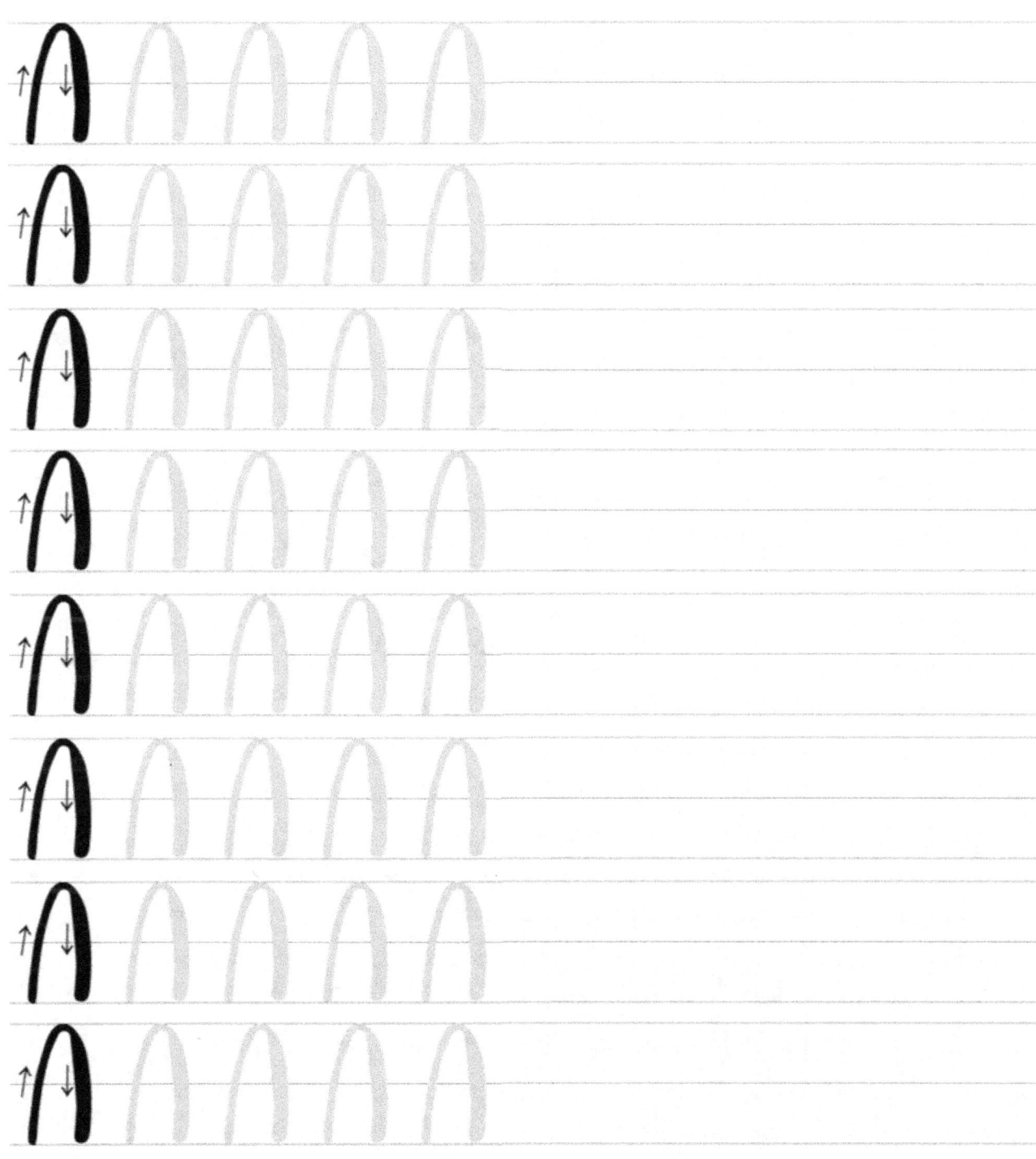

BASIC STROKES

Over Turns

Now try it one more time without de gray line. Let's practice.

TIPS ABOUT CALLIGRAPHY

Here I bring you some additional tips to consider before you start. Always remember that the basic concepts are really important.

Hold the pen correctly, it is essential to accommodate the pen in a way that your muscles won't suffer and that will allow you to get the most out of each and single stroke. Beware to hold the pen creating unnecessary tension in your hand.

Have a good posture, sit straight, keep the writing surface in front of you (not to far and not to close) and have plenty of room for your arm to move – your whole forearm should be touching the surface of the table.

Lift the pen after each stroke, this will help you with the consistency and with the precision of your strokes.

Stop comparing yourself, leave these expectations behind and learn how to be curious and have fun just like a child. Being relaxed and confident are the perfect combo for learning and perfecting a new skill such this one.

But also remember enjoy the ride and let the art flow through your hands. You have so much creativity on yourself that it's time the world see it.

2
TO THE NEXT LEVEL

CHOOSING A LETTERING STYLE

You have to know all the different styles so you can choose the one that fits your current project the best. Knowing the basic styles will help you create endless variations of the same letter.

The most important thing to keep in mind at all times is legibility. You can create the most ornate, fancy looking E, but if it can't be easily recognized as an E you failed.

Serif lettering: A serif is the small line attached at the end of a letter's stroke. Within this category, there are many other styles. We've got old style serifs, transitional serifs, modern serifs, glyphic serifs or slab serifs.

Sans serif lettering: "Sans" means without. So this category of lettering contains typography that has no lines attached to the ends of each letterform. Sans serif lettering is often used to convey a more contemporary style.

Even though these letterforms have a more basic structure than serifs, there are still a number of creative ways to do this.

Script and brush lettering: Script and brush lettering refers to letterforms that are connected to each other. This can be very formal looking and elegant o playful. This style imitates calligraphy, but instead of drawing the letters with a single movement of the hand like you would in calligraphy, you draw the letters from many little pencil strokes to build that look.

The most important rule to keep in mind is that a letter's upstroke is always thin, and its downstroke is always thick. Up thin, down thick. You minimize the pressure of the pen on the ups, you push and create more pressure on the downs. Up thin, down thick. Up thin, down thick.

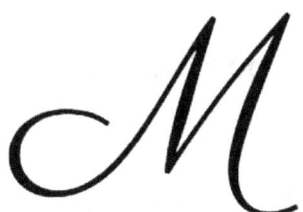

BOOST YOUR LETTERING SKILLS

Before you start, there are few terms you should become familiar with and a few terms you should remember from the last section:

- **Cap line:** The guiding line that establishes the height for all capital letters.

- **X-line:** The guiding line that establishes the height for all lowercase letters.

- **Baseline:** The guiding line upon which the entire word or phrase sits on.

- **Flourish:** Flourishes are decorative strokes that can be added to letters to provide movement. The key is to maintain balance in order to create an elegant look. Flourishes include loops and swirls.

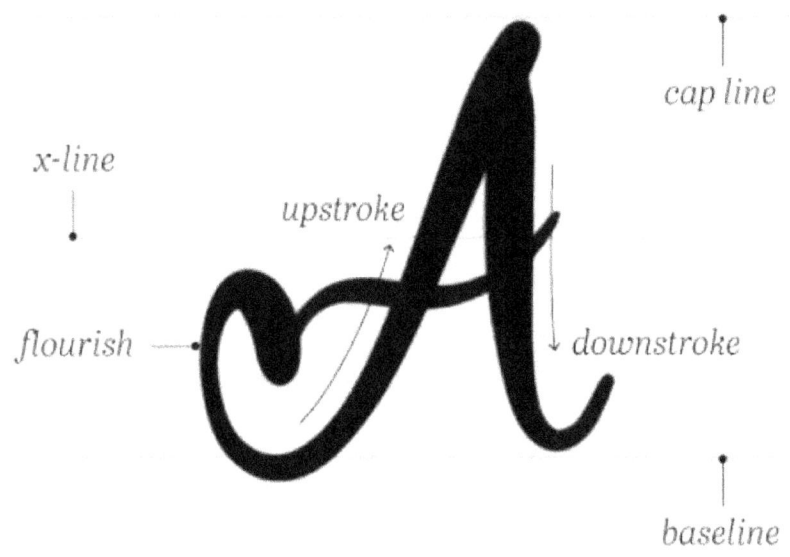

The key to mastering the art of hand lettering is practice. Use all the beautiful temples in this book as a reference guide, which includes all the letters of the alphabet, to help you hone your hand lettering skills.

Here are a few pointers to keep in mind while you practice your hand lettering skills:

o   Release pressure on upstrokes to create thin lines.

o   Apply pressure on down strokes to create thick lines.

o   Stray outside of the guiding lines to achieve a more dynamic look.

o   Play with loops and flourishes once you've mastered the basics.

BASIC STROKES

More shapes and Turns

Now try it connecting strokes. Let's practice.

BASIC STROKES

More shapes and Turns

Now try it connecting strokes. Let's practice.

BASIC STROKES

More shapes and Turns

Now try it connecting strokes. Let's practice.

uuuu

uuuu

uuuu

uuuu

uuuu

uuuu

uuuu

BASIC STROKES

More shapes and Turns

Now try it connecting strokes. Let's practice.

llll

llll

llll

llll

llll

llll

llll

BASIC STROKES

More shapes and Turns

Now try it connecting strokes. Let's practice.

3
YOUR FIRST LETTERS

BASIC ALPHABET - UPPERCASE

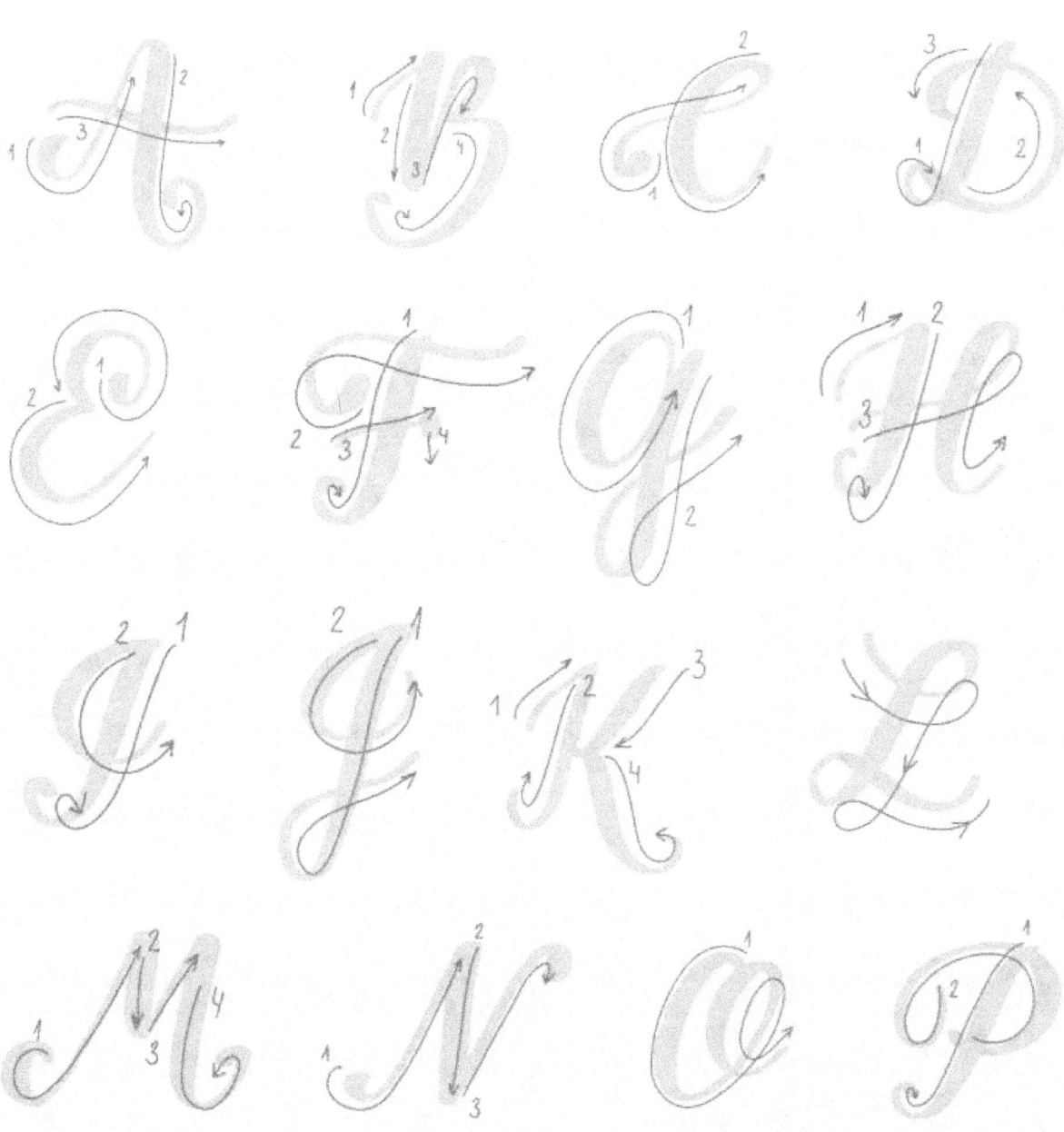

BASIC ALPHABET – UPPERCASE

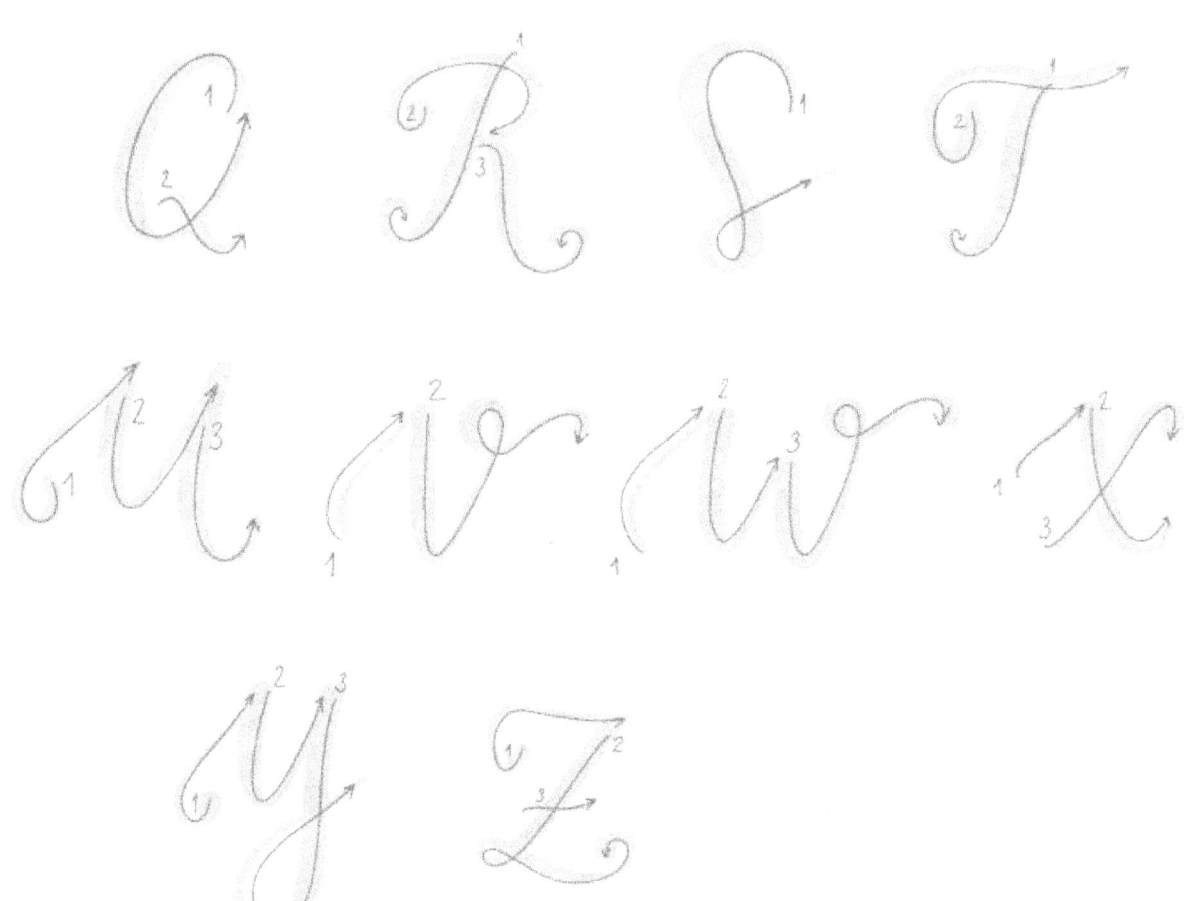

BASIC ALPHABET - UPPERCASE

A

B

C

D

E

BASIC ALPHABET - UPPERCASE

BASIC ALPHABET – UPPERCASE

55

BASIC ALPHABET – UPPERCASE

57

BASIC ALPHABET - UPPERCASE

59

BASIC ALPHABET – UPPERCASE

BASIC ALPHABET - LOWERCASE

BASIC ALPHABET - LOWERCASE

a

b

c

d

e

f

BASIC ALPHABET - LOWERCASE

I left you more space between lines in order you feel free to take the space you need. Let's practice.

BASIC ALPHABET - LOWERCASE

I left you more space between lines in order you feel free to take the space you need. Let's practice.

BASIC ALPHABET - LOWERCASE

I left you more space between lines in order you feel free to take the space you need. Let's practice.

BASIC ALPHABET - LOWERCASE

4
MORE FUN LETTERS

NEW FUN STYLE 1

Aa Aa   Bb Bb
Cc Cc   Dd Dd
Ee Ee   Ff Ff
Gg Gg   Hh Hh
Ii Ii   Jj Jj
Kk Kk   Ll Ll
Mm Mm   Nn Nn
Oo Oo   Pp Pp
Qq Qq   Rr Rr

NEW FUN STYLE 1

Ss Ss   Tt Tt
Uu Uu   Vv Vv
Ww Ww   Xx Xx
Yy Yy   Zz Zz

Numbers:

11 11   22 22   33 33
44 44   55 55   66 66
77 77   88 88   99 99

NEW FUN STYLE 2

Aa Aa   Bb Bb
Cc Cc   Dd Dd
Ee Ee   Ff Ff
Gg Gg   Hh Hh
Ii Ii   Jj Jj
Kk Kk   Ll Ll
Mm Mm   Nn Nn
Oo Oo   Pp Pp
Qq Qq   Rr Rr

NEW FUN STYLE 2

Ss Ss   Tt Tt

Uu Uu   Vv Vv

Ww Ww   Xx Xx

Yy Yy   Zz Zz

Numbers:

11 11   22 22   33 33

44 44   55 55   66 66

77 77   88 88   99 99

NEW FUN STYLE 3

Aa Aa   Bb Bb

Cc Cc   Dd Dd

Ee Ee   Ff Ff

Gg Gg   Hh Hh

Ii Ii   Jj Jj

Kk Kk   Ll Ll

Mm Mm   Nn Nn

Oo Oo   Pp Pp

Qq Qq   Rr Rr

NEW FUN STYLE 3

Ss Ss Tt Tt

Uu Uu Vv Vv

Ww Ww Xx Xx

Yy Yy Zz Zz

Numbers:

11 11 22 22 33 33

44 44 55 55 66 66

77 77 88 88 99 99

5
UNLEASH YOUR CREATIVITY

ORNAMENTAL ELEMENTS

Let's learn how to do some ornamental elements. Look the patterns:

Now do it for yourself! Follow the gray pattern as a guide and go beyond that:

ORNAMENTAL ELEMENTS

Let's learn how to do some ornamental elements. Look the patterns:

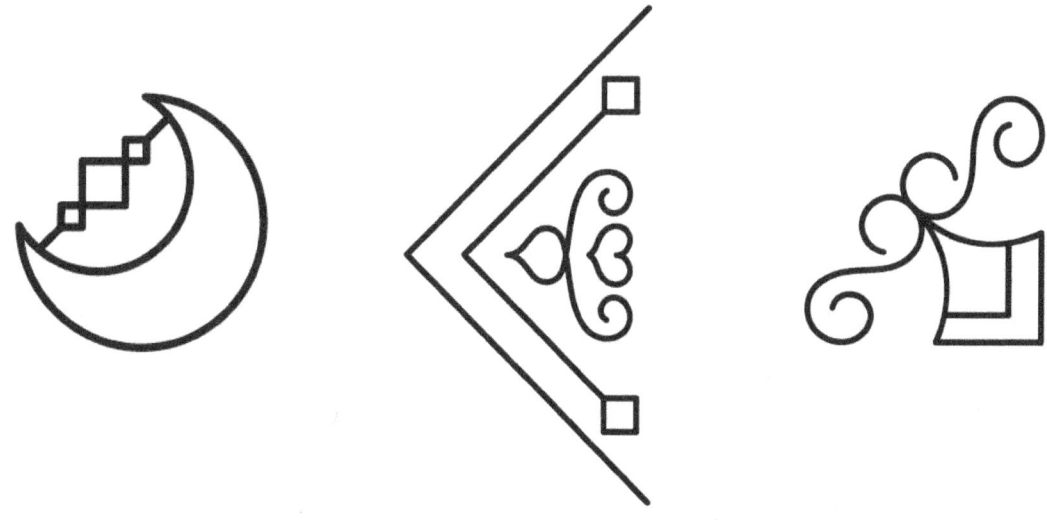

Now do it for yourself! Follow the gray pattern as a guide and go beyond that:

ORNAMENTAL ELEMENTS

Let's learn how to do some ornamental elements. Look the patterns:

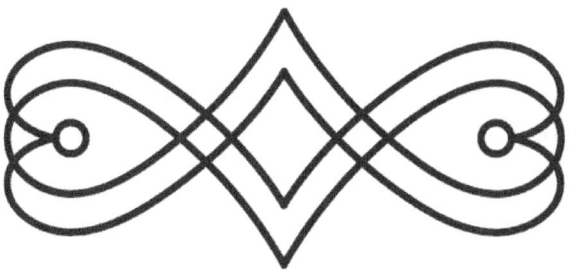

Now do it for yourself! Follow the gray pattern as a guide and go beyond that:

ORNAMENTAL ELEMENTS

Let's learn how to do some ornamental elements. Look the patterns:

Now do it for yourself! Follow the gray pattern as a guide and go beyond that:

ADD DETAILS AND CREATIVITY

Add some **details** on the letters themselves. Add anything from a simple inline to intricate flourishes and shading.

Add decorative elements to fill the empty space around your letters. Again, keep the letters readable at all times. Flourishes and swashes can be part of your letters or stand on their own. Either way, they can help balance out your composition and make your letters stand out.

Draw expressive letterforms expressing feelings and emotions solely with the style of the drawn letters. Practice by trying to illustrate random words with the help of letters. Pick your word and think about what feelings can that word evoke.

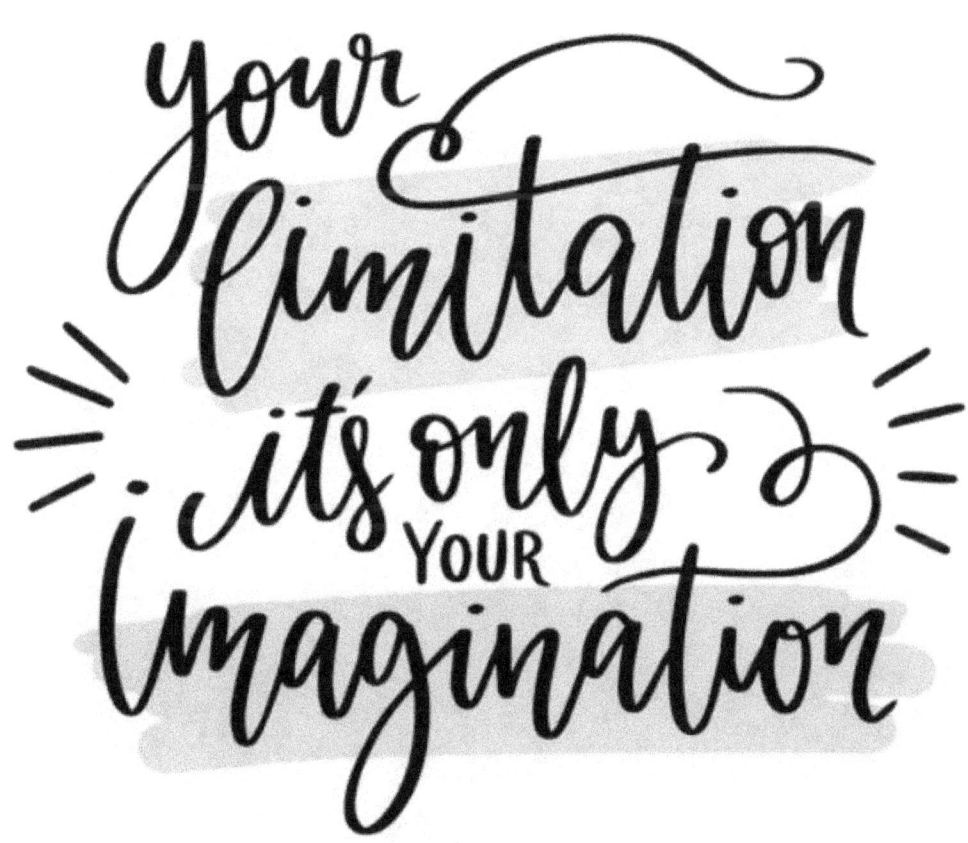

MORE DESIGNS

Look at the next design and try to trace the pattern in the next page. Remember enjoy the process.

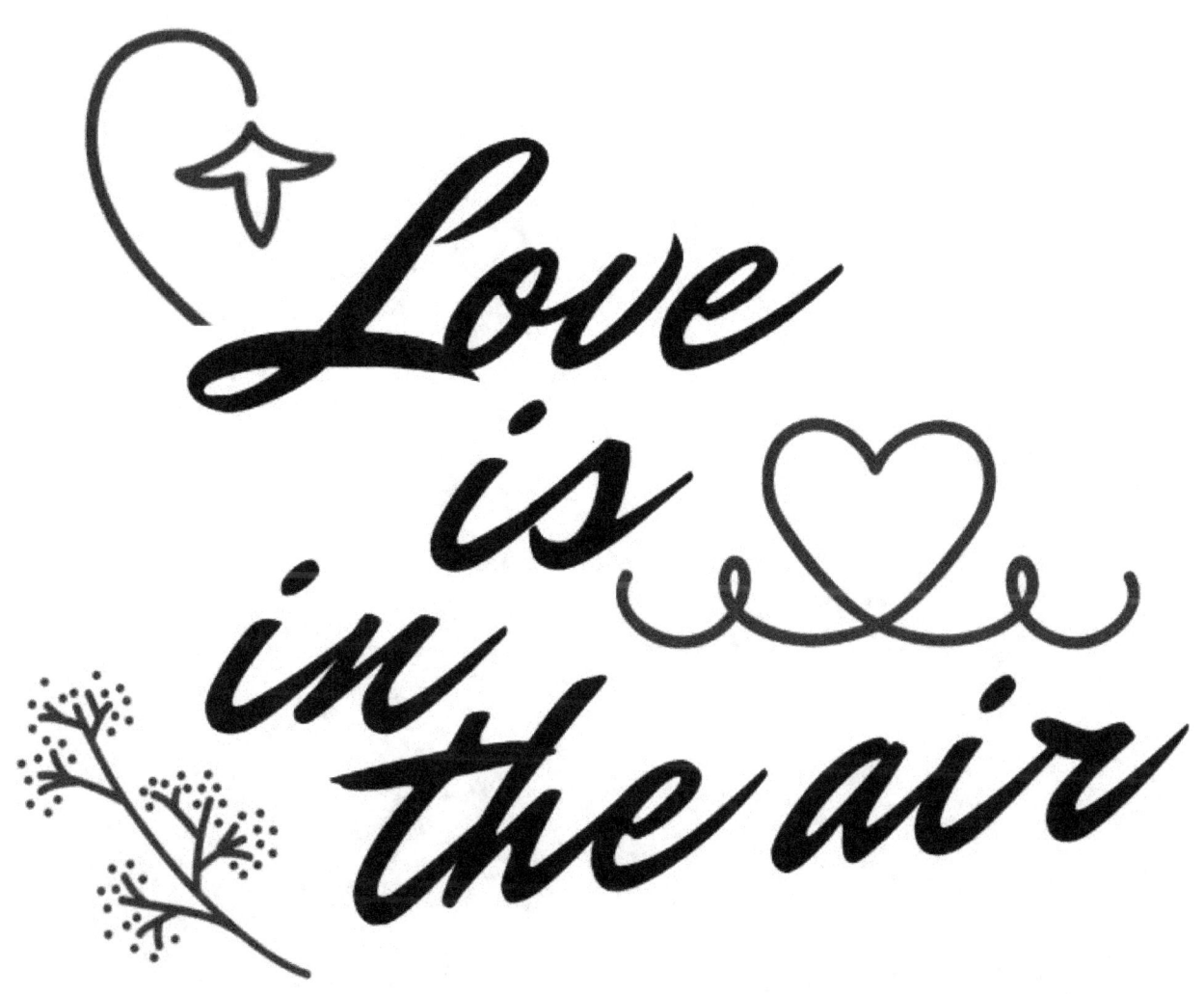

MORE DESIGNS

Now do it for yourself! Release your creativity!

MORE DESIGNS

Look at the next design and try to trace the pattern in the next page. Remember enjoy the process.

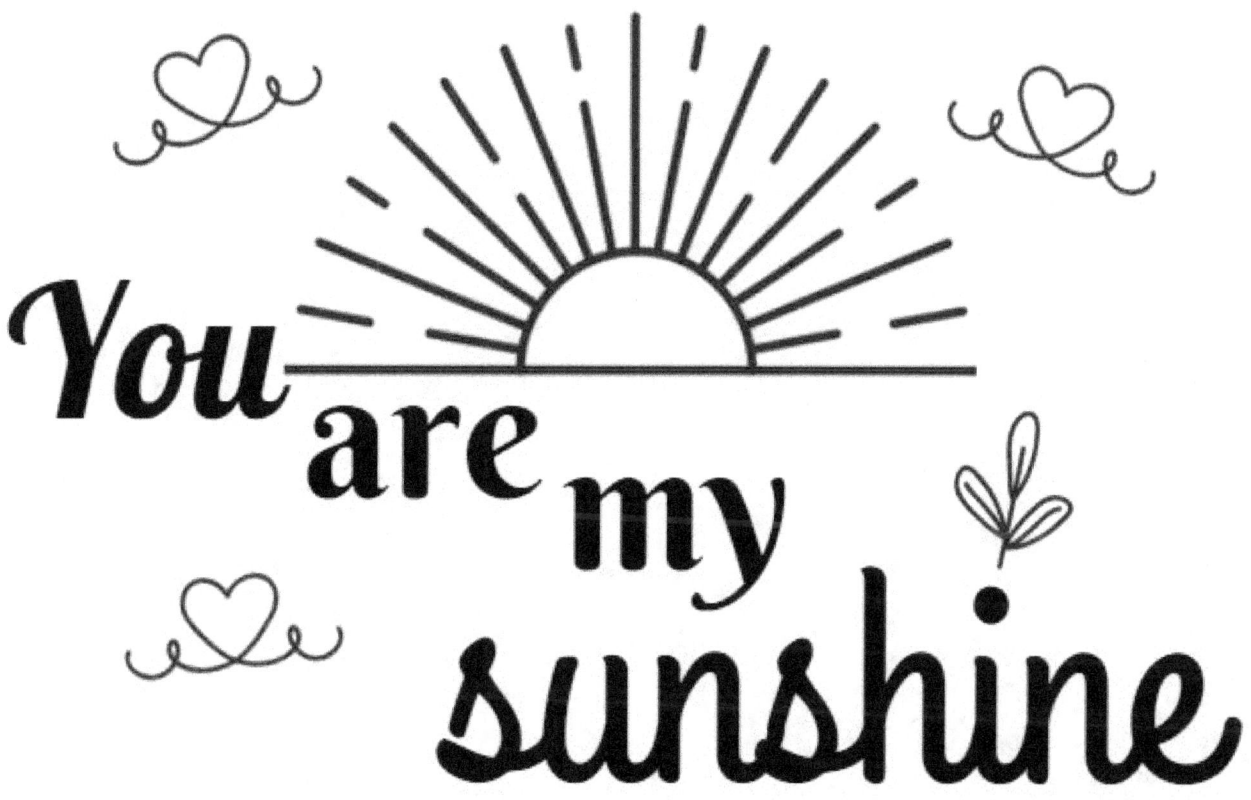

MORE DESIGNS

Now do it for yourself! Release your creativity!

CONCLUSION

Thank you so much for your purchase, and I would like to tell you that I am very happy to help you take your first steps on this amazing journey.

If you enjoyed this book, then please leave an Amazon review. Reviews are the lifeblood of our publishing endeavors, and leaving a review would mean the world to us.

Thanks again!

Charlotte Robinson
TFC Guide Publishing

Available now on Amazon

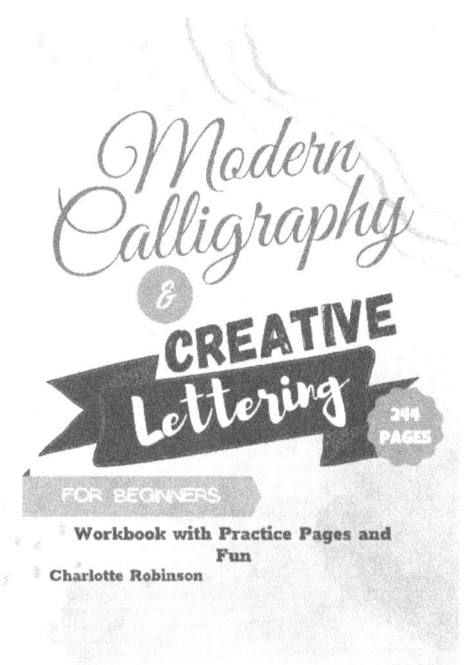 

PAPERBACK ASIN: B08DSX3J9J

This "**Modern Calligraphy and Creative Lettering for beginners: Workbook with Practice Pages and Fun**" is a complementary workbook, which contains:
- Templates to practice the basic strokes.
- Basic alphabet with uppercase and lowercase templates.
- Ten beautiful styles of letters (including an alphabet, numbers, words and positive phrases).
- More than 180 great words and phrases, and designs of the lettering art to practice and have fun.

JUST A QUICK FAVOR...

Please you feel free to send us any comment or suggestion through the next channels:

Email: admin@tfcguide.com

Please write us by email and we will send you more digital templates as a gift, so you can continue practicing and perfecting the styles shown.

Our goal is to improve and create more valuable books for you.

Thanks again!

Charlotte Robinson
TFC Guide Publishing

ACKNOWLEDGEMENTS

I would also like to thank the valuable contribution of these people who inspired the creation of this book:

- Timo Ostrich
- Pat from Paspartú
- Marvy Uchida
- Krystal Whitten

Thanks again!

Charlotte Robinson
TFC Guide Publishing

More books by Charlotte Robinson

www.ingramcontent.com/pod-product-compliance
Lightning Source LLC
Chambersburg PA
CBHW080502220526
45465CB00006B/2347